ONE MINUTE SUNSOFT SOLARIS MANAGER

By the
OnWord Press Development Team
with M. C. Burns

ONE MINUTE SUNSOFT SOLARIS MANAGER

By the OnWord Press Development Team with M. C. Burns

Published by:

OnWord Press
1580 Center Drive
Santa Fe NM 87505 USA

All rights reserved. No part of this book may be reproduced or transmitted in any form or by any means, electronic or mechanical, including photocopying, recording or by any information storage and retrieval system without written permission from the publisher, except for the inclusion of brief quotations in a review.

Copyright © 1993 OnWord Press

10 9 8 7 6 5 4 3 2 1

Printed in the United States of America

Library of Congress Cataloging-in-Publication Data

OnWord Press Development Team, Burns, M.C.

One Minute SunSoft Solaris Manager

1.Solaris 2. System Management I. Title

92-61881

ISBN 0-934605-81-5

Trademarks

OnWord Press is a trademark of High Mountain Press. Any other products and services mentioned in this book are either trademarks or registered trademarks of their respective companies. OnWord Press and the authors make no claim to these marks.

Warning and Disclaimer

This book is designed to provide information about system management. Every effort has been made to make this book complete and as accurate as possible; however, no warranty or fitness is implied.

The information is provided on an "as-is" basis. The authors and OnWord Press shall have neither liability nor responsibility to any person or entity with respect to any loss or damages in connection with or rising from the information contained in this book.

About the Authors

The OnWord Press Development Team is a group of skilled and conscientious editors and writers.

Special Thanks

Thanks to John Salas, Scott Cook, Stephen Goodwin, and Scott Deshaies for their technical advice and review.

Book Production

This book was produced using Ventura 4.1 Desktop Publishing software running on 80386 and 80486 PCs. Text was produced with a variety of word processing programs. Illustrations were produced by John Tollett with Adobe Illustrator on a Mac IIci.

OnWord Press.....

OnWord Press is dedicated to the fine art of practical software user's documentation.

In addition to the authors who developed the material for this book, other members of the OnWord Press team make the book end up in your hands.

Thanks to David Talbott, Dan Raker, Frank Conforti, Gary Cascio, John Tollett, Clint Hicks, Scott Deshaies, Carol Leyba, Patrice Werner, Lynne Eigensteiner, and the numerous other members of the OnWord Press team who contributed to the production and distribution of this book.

Introduction

The *One Minute Solaris Manager* is a fast paced book for anyone seeking or being pushed into a system management role. This light volume presents anecdotes, tips and suggestions in a dozen basic strategies for becoming an effective network manager.

Underlying themes include the use of four basic tools to transform yourself from a totally dependent member of the organization to a strong, responsible team player. These four tools are recognition, education, delegation and communication.

Lively, true life anecdotes illustrate essential points in each chapter. Note that names of people and places have been changed to protect the innocent.

Finally, the *One Minute Solaris Manager* is intended to help you develop as a system manager and become a more valuable member of your enterprise. In the end you must rely on your own skills, knowledge and abilities to be a successful system manager.

"I know of no more encouraging fact than the unquestionable ability of man to elevate his life by a conscious endeavor."
—Henry David Thoreau

Table of Contents

Introduction v

SECTION 1–Understanding Your Needs

1–Recognizing Your Need For Job Security 5

2–The Need For Recognition 13

3–The Need For Time 21

4–The Need For Job Satisfaction 31

SECTION 2–Developing Yourself

5–Understanding Your Own Personal Motivation 39

6–The Need For Personal Development 45

7–Technical Mastery Is a Myth 55

8–Leadership: The Ultimate Act of Independence 61

SECTION 3–Developing The Team

9–Helping Others Manage 69

10–Being An Effective Team Player 77

11–Implementing It All 85

12–Contributing to Corporate Goals and Success 93

ONE MINUTE SUNSOFT SOLARIS MANAGER

*By the
OnWord Press Development Team
with M. C. Burns*

Section 1

Understanding Your Needs

There is a period in everyone's working life when all you have is given to you by others. You have ideas, perhaps good ideas, and commitment. But all you can do is attend to what is dumped on your plate. We call this the "They" phase, because your life revolves around what "they" give you to do. Recognition, delegation, communication, and education comes from or through others.

The goal of this section is to work toward becoming independent of others by relying on yourself to establish a sense of job security, receive recognition for your labors, manage your time and find job satisfaction.

Chapter 1

Recognizing Your Need For Job Security

"No one can make you inferior without your consent." — Eleanor Roosevelt

Is the Grass Truly Greener?

One Monday morning you walk into your office. Before you put down your coffee and check your E-mail, your boss walks in and says, "I'd like you to meet Joe Howard. We're talking to him about coming on board as another system manager. We heard you when you said you needed more staff to get the job done."

You clench your teeth in a kind of smile and say, "Great, that's great. Nice to meet you."

They leave and you wonder why they didn't hear you when you said you needed an assistant, not another system manager.

You walk down the hall to see how the engineers are doing on the research project, trying to forget Joe Howard and focus on the work in front of you.

"Hey, how's it going this morning? Any more error messages?"

"Oh, didn't you hear?" asks one of the engineers. "The project has been put on hold and we've been reassigned to the Galen project. Weren't you in on that meeting?"

Feelings of paranoia rise up from your stomach and you say, "No. Why was the project put on hold?"

"They decided we don't have the staff or equipment to put the time into it now. They may start up again after some changes are made. There's even talk again about layoffs."

You go back to your office wondering how you got so far out of the loop. If their were questions about equipment, why didn't they ask you? Why is management hiring a new system manager at the same time they are thinking about layoffs?

You login to your machine and check your E-mail. A message from the head of engineering. Good; this must be the message informing you of the change in project status.

The message reads, "I hear from Bill that the new networking system still isn't in place. I thought I told you that it had to be in place by the 5th so we could begin data transfers between buildings."

You reply, "There are still a few bugs in the system in the other building. It should be up by the 9th."

Not only are you out of the information loop, but others aren't being kept informed of your activities. You've done your part by getting the system ready to go in your building, but what management will remember about the project was that it was late.

You've been hearing that the Acme Research Company is looking for a good system manager and they know how to treat their staff well.

You decide it's time to update your resume and get your three-piece suit cleaned.

Recognizing Your Need for Job Security

Everyone has a deep rooted, fundamental need for job security. It is also true that nearly everyone entertains some level of insecurity at one time or another in their careers.

Some people ignore their fears about job security, preferring to bluff and bluster their way along. Others simply live in fear, seeing every deed of their colleagues as a trick, a plot to unseat, an undermining coup in the making.

If you have ever thought about any of the following issues, you have encountered the problem of job security:

- Is the company stable? Will I be laid off in 6 months, or sooner?

- Is my work adequate? Do I know enough to do my job?

- My efforts help everybody, yet I don't get recognition for my work.

- I'm an engineer, not a manager. What am I supposed to do in a management role?

- If I teach people everything I know, will I still be needed?

- It is so much easier to do it myself rather than take the time to explain it to somebody else.
- The boss does not really understand what I do and therefore makes uninformed decisions.
- Everyone around here thinks they can be the system manager.

Don't Just Seek Job Security—Create It

Job security is not something you find lying under a rock or hidden in a closet, nor is it something lying about at the company across the street. It is largely the product of your own labors.

If you take possession of your job, claim it as your own and take responsibility for your decisions and your labors, job security will follow.

If you take the time to understand the direction in which your organization is going, listen to the needs of those around you, and use your skills to the best of your ability, job security will chase you down.

If you do these things and manage effectively as well so that you pass on the spirit of responsibility and conscientiousness to others, your labors will strengthen the entire organization. Job security will overtake you.

Freeing Yourself With Your Knowledge and Expertise

Your strongest ally in any management situation is your own body of knowledge and skills. You would not be in the position you are in if somebody did not recognize something of value in you.

Use your knowledge and skills. Grow to rely on them. Develop and expand them. Allow others to benefit from what you posses.

The surest way to both use and expand upon your knowledge and skills is to share them freely with others. Everything you do and say will not always be right. Thank God for that, because not knowing and being in error is the first step to growing beyond yourself.

Summary

☐ Everyone has a fundamental need for job security, and that's OK.

☐ Recognizing this need will in itself provide a sense of security as a nucleus around which to build job stability.

☐ Listen to the needs of others so that your labors are useful to the organization.

☐ Recognize that your closest ally is your own knowledge and expertise.

☐ By openly sharing your knowledge and expertise, you free yourself to tackle new opportunities and new challenges—to grow into ever more secure positions.

Chapter 2

The Need For Recognition

"The deepest principle of Human Nature is the craving to be appreciated." –William James

"The trouble with most of us is that we would rather be ruined by praise than saved by criticism." –Norman Vincent Peale

Up Against the Ceiling

At the latest staff meeting it was agreed that a proposal to solve the security problem needed to be written. You and a coworker have been assigned to research and present the proposal.

For the next week, in between systems crashing and restoring files, you and your coworker investigate how to stop intruders from using the system to hide software that others then call in to download.

You pass your boss in the hall.

"Have you had a chance to install the new E-mail system yet?" she asks.

"No, I haven't. I understood the security break was top priority this week, but I'll install the new E-mail right away."

"O.K., great."

You go back to your office and figure out how and when to install the new system. It will mean working late several nights, but you can get it done this week.

The next day you pass the director of engineering in the hall.

"I've been meaning to ask you," he says, "Have you written the new hardware and software report yet? We need that report this week for the budgeting meeting."

"I'll get it finished up right away," you reply, visualizing another long night.

The Need For Recognition

You and your coworker still haven't gotten very far on the security problem, but it's one of those weeks and somehow you'll get it all done.

You close your office door and make some phone calls before getting back to work on the software report.

The phone rings. "Hey, the server's screwing up. We're getting weird error messages."

You stop to figure out the problem Several hours later you get back to the software report.

Your coworker sticks her head in the door. "We have to get to that security problem. I have to leave at 5:00 tonight, so can we work on it now?"

You stop what you're doing and go to work. A couple hours work and you have figured out how to block hackers a little better and to track incoming calls on the modem.

Another long, hard day's work, but tomorrow you'll have the security proposal together and the proposal for next year's hardware purchases. The new E-mail system will be up with a few more hours' work.

Bright and early the next morning you bring the budget proposal into the office of the director of engineering.

"I have the report he wanted," you tell his assistant.

"He's out of town. Decided to go to a conference at the last minute. The budget meeting was postponed."

You shrug and leave. At least you did your part.

Later at the staff meeting you prepare to present your security ideas. The staff gets into a discussion on stress and they never get to your report.

"Next week," they say.

The Need for Recognition

Lack of recognition is a fundamental cause of job dissatisfaction and insecurity. Have you ever felt confused about whether your work is of any value, or do you feel taken for granted? You need RECOGNITION.

Unfortunately, we often fail to identify our need of recognition. It is not selfish to desire recognition. Everyone needs recognition for work well done. For most of us this is the only way we know we are of value in the organization. Recognition is OK.

Recognition comes in many forms. It can be a pat on the back, a memo, a financial reward, a special bonus, even a promotion.

It must also come from the right places. Just because the cleaning crew thinks you are a hard worker because they see you every night doesn't necessarily quench your need for recognition.

Getting the Recognition You Need and Deserve

The key to receiving recognition is to know what you need and then make your needs known to those who are important to you.

What kind of recognition do you need? It is essential that you answer this question. You must know your needs so that you can communicate them to others and identify recognition when you receive it.

For most people recognition is not simply money or awards or position. It is a combination of things that establish you as a significant person in the organization.

How do you gain recognition from those whose opinions matter? Communicate your needs and your accomplishments. Recognition will not happen if you hide the fruits of your labors. In most cases, a simple conversation will go a long way toward eliminating misunderstandings on this point.

Putting Your Accomplishments In Perspective

Do not confuse praise for a job well done with just doing your job. Showing up to work every day is what you get paid to do.

Expect recognition for goals achieved, special problems solved and outstanding application of your knowledge and skills.

Summary

☐ Accept your craving for recognition. It is natural and everyone needs it.

☐ Recognition comes in many forms. Understand what kind of recognition you need.

☐ Communicate needs for recognition; communicate appreciation of recognition when it is received.

☐ Reality check—put your accomplishments in perspective.

☐ Some people are not good at giving recognition; acknowledge this when you are giving and receiving it.

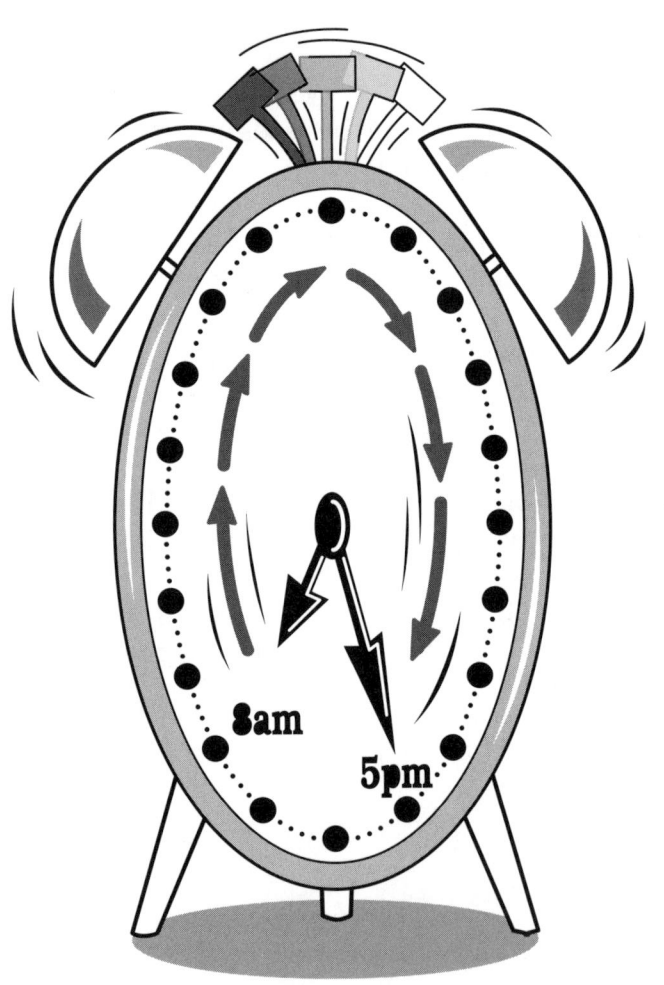

Chapter 3

The Need For Time

"Never put off until tomorrow what you can do the day after tomorrow." –Mark Twain

"Work expands so as to fill the time available for its completion." –Northcote Parkinson

"Work expands so as to exceed the time available for its completion." –Dan Raker

"Time is nature's way of keeping everything from happening at once." –Unknown

Life in an Infinitely Expanding Universe

You sit down at your desk, papers scattered everywhere and your to-do list on the screen. It reads like this:

- Answer questions on E-mail

One Minute SunSoft Solaris Manager

- Return in-house phone calls
- Track down data-corruption bug
- Partial back-up day
- Get the new printer on-line
- Figure out why NFS server went off line
- Trouble shoot CAD user environment
- Clear old files off server
- Fill out expense report
- Install new memory boards
- Restore trashed file

You decide to restore the file because it's holding other people up. Before you can get out the door, the phone rings.

"Hi. It's Miriam. We have a minor problem with the bulletin board. Do you have a few minutes to take a look at it?"

"Sure," you say, "I'll be right there."

The Need For Time

A couple of minutes turns into 45 minutes before you're heading back down the hall to fix the trashed file.

You run into Harry on the way.

"Did you hear?" he asks. "We're going to need you to shut down the server for a while and help us track down the source of some errors.

"O.K. When?"

Well, now of course."

An hour and a half later you get back to your office and go immediately to your E-mail, which you haven't had a chance to check yet.

There are several urgent messages: a printer is malfunctioning in the administration office; someone can't get an application to work; and the new database system is threatening to quit working altogether.

It will take all day to get these things straightened out. But wait, what's this? A top priority E-mail from the head of accounting about a massive data loss.

The phone rings. It's your boss.

"Come over right away. I'm expecting some important information through Internet and I can't get into E-mail."

You say you'll be right there.

The phone rings again. It's your boss' boss.

"Come over right away," he says. "Our system manager is out sick and the network has crashed."

You're pretty sure you'll explode at the rate demands are being made on you, so you stop, take a breath, and, singing happy songs, head over to your boss' office on the way to fixing the network. It takes you through lunch and well into the afternoon before the network is up again.

You make it back to your office, ready for the emergency corn nuts you have stashed for when you miss lunch. The head of accounting has been leaving messages for you every quarter hour about recovering the data.

You swallow the nuts and walk over to the accounting department, stopped only once on the way by a user with a work-threatening problem.

Does Time Control You or Do You Control Time?

An important aspect of becoming an effective manager is gaining control of your own schedule. Without this skill, you are hard pressed to accomplish either your professional or personal goals.

Time Is Yours—Take It

Your time is a valuable finite personal resource. If you do not take and use it, somebody else will. How do others use your time? They do it when you let them. Here are some of the ways you let others steal your time:

- People dump their problems on you and you let them;

- You promise the impossible to please your supervisor;

- You promise the impossible because you want to convince yourself an difficult task is smaller than it really is;

- You allow other people's emergencies to become your priorities;

- Tasks grow to fill or exceed the time allotted for them through finely honed work avoidance techniques.

Take Back Your Time and Keep It

The first step in taking possession of your own time is recognizing that it is yours to control. Then you must allocate it as you see fit.

Sometimes this involves balancing priorities and making hard choices. After all, you do have obligations and responsibilities to others in your work group and to the company. You have a limited supply of time while the world around you has unlimited needs for it. If you allow others to make your choices, you are not in control, and you are not managing.

How do you take control and manage your time? Consider some of these techniques:

- Be ruthlessly realistic in your time estimates. Do not try to please your supervisor or fool yourself by promising too much. Do not avoid work by promising too little.

The Need For Time

- Learn to balance priorities. Part of working effectively in an organization is understanding how you can best contribute to goals. When confronted with conflicting demands on your time, do what you do best and delegate the rest.

- Delegation of responsibility is not copping out. It is the only way for you to take back the time you need to do what you cannot delegate. Understanding your own need for time is an essential prerequisite to knowing how to manage yourself, delegate responsibility and manage others. You will hear more about this as you read on.

One Minute SunSoft Solaris Manager

Summary

☐ Recognize your need to be in control of your time and be aggressive about controlling your time.

☐ Your time problems become other people's time problems, and their time problems become yours.

☐ Do not take on other people's responsibilities out of pity for their plight. Educate them, delegate, but do not do their work for them.

☐ Do not overcommit yourself just to please everybody. You will please nobody.

☐ Complete work in time rather than fill time with work.

The Need For Time

Chapter 4

The Need For Job Satisfaction

"I cannot believe that the purpose of life is to be "happy." I think the purpose of life is to be useful, to be responsible, to be honorable, to be compassionate. It is, above all, to matter: to count, to stand for something, to have made some difference that you lived."
–Leo C. Rosten

Are We Having Fun Yet?

What a week. There was the usual maintenance work to be done: cleaning out junk files on the servers, and some unusual maintenance: fixing wiring messes.

There were the special projects to do: installing the software upgrade and reworking some coding standards.

There were the usual questions and problems: someone's monitor went dead ("Did you check the wires?" you asked. "No....Should I?"); someone got insulted by an error message ("It called me a spasmodic, and then I swear it laughed at me."); a process kept freezing and had to be killed, repeatedly.

When the plumbing backed up and the ensuing flood threatened a server and several hard drives, you were right there, directing the rescue and keeping everyone on-line.

Your boss congratulated you on the solutions you had to the security problem; a rare compliment.

You helped the engineering department get plans out on a big project. "Way to go," you said to one of the engineers.

"Getting that project out was miserable," he replied, "and now we just have to get back to the 50 million other projects due in the next month."

It's the end of a long week. Even though you did not get to planning the new configuration for the system, you are feeling pretty good. You have gotten a good amount of work done and are looking forward to tackling next week's work, after the weekend that is.

The Need for Job Satisfaction

People respond differently to a given set of circumstances, but there is one thing everyone has in common. To be effective at what they do, people must derive satisfaction from what they do.

You are no exception. Job satisfaction is not just a blissful state that hopefully you will experience one day. Striving for and finding job satisfaction enables you to excel at what you do.

What Makes Job Satisfaction

There are many factors that contribute to job satisfaction. Different people value them differently. A very important part of becoming an effective manager is understanding what gives you satisfaction in your work. Which one or ones is it?

- Recognition by peers and others;

- Accomplishment;
- Meeting the challenge;
- Money;
- Career advancement;
- Personal security.

The "Grass Is Greener" Syndrome

One of the most common urges that you must confront in yourself and others is the sense that everything would be better if only you were someplace else. However, when you experience it, you must ask yourself if it is real.

REALITY CHECK: When you start looking for a better position, are you pursuing job satisfaction or escaping your own weaknesses? The answer may not be finding another job so much as becoming more effective in the one you have.

Creating Job Satisfaction Out of Dissatisfaction

Dissatisfaction is an internal warning that something is not right. Rather than turning away from it, confront it and use it to identify your needs. Then pursue them.

Not only is there nothing wrong with actively pursuing what satisfies you, but you have an obligation to do so in order to be most effective in your organization.

Summary

☐ Recognize you have a craving for job satisfaction and that to be most effective in your work, you must satisfy that craving.

☐ Understand where your job satisfaction comes from and that not everyone achieves job satisfaction in the same way.

☐ Do not turn away from job dissatisfaction, but confront it and use it to develop an understanding of what satisfies you.

☐ Actively pursue job satisfaction in a way that makes you competent and confident in what you do.

Section 2

Developing Yourself

Once you have recognized your basic needs and developed confidence in your ability to satisfy them, you have graduated to what we call the "Me" phase. Here you begin to control recognition, education, communication, and delegation to become independent and confident in your work.

The goal of this section is to learn how to sustain yourself so that you can become a manager who can pass on these essentials to others. We stress educating yourself about what motivates you, about the importance of personal development and growth, about gaining confidence in technical mastery and finally becoming a leader.

Chapter 5

Understanding Your Own Personal Motivation

"We know nothing about motivation. All we can do is write books about it."
–Peter Drucker

To Do or Not To Do

Your company is expanding to another floor of the building. The departments are being split, and you and the other system administrator have decided when and how to set up the new network.

It occurs to you that now is the time to set up broadcast addresses and some subnetwork masks between the servers. The question is when will you have the time? You begin by taking an hour here and there to set up the machines into their logical configurations.

The move to the other floor is made, and you and the other system administrator get the system up and running after a number of problems are worked out.

You continue on your own, sometimes in the evenings, to get the network masks in place. It takes longer than expected. Few people know what you are doing, and most will not notice the performance gains your address scheme will achieve.

Finally it's done and you send out your first packet. It's working well. You feel your work was worth it when performance tests indicate a more efficient configuration, even with the expanded network.

What Motivates You?

Are you terrified of being fired? Are you striving for a promotion? Do you want more money? Are you motivated by a challenge? Do you want to participate meaningfully in a group effort? Are you competing with your peers?

Perhaps you are simply motivated by the desire to never have more than five items on your to-do list.

Personal achievement and recognition for your accomplishments may be the foundation of job satisfaction and security. However, motivation is what makes personal achievement possible.

Positive and Negative Motivators

Most people are driven by a complex of motivating forces. Some are positive and some are negative.

Positive motivational forces are those that attract you, such as meeting a challenge, gaining personal recognition or contributing to a common goal. Negative motivators are those that repel you, such as fear of losing your job.

Do not let negative motivators take over your life. When you are bombarded with tasks all day long (and you are), you begin to resent having to perform these tasks. This can send you on the slippery slope of apathy and resentment of your job.

When looking at the tasks you perform you should look for the positive motivators that will allow you to complete the task with that warm and fuzzy feeling.

Summary

- ☐ Know what motivates you. Look for those hidden motivators.

- ☐ Self-worth is a component of personal motivation—you can't do anything if you don't believe the value of what you do.

- ☐ You are your own primary motivator.

- ☐ Recognize when a negative motivator is having an effect on your performance and change it.

Chapter 6

The Need For Personal Development

"Never say you don't know—nod wisely, leave calmly, then run like hell to find the nearest expert." –S.M. Oddo

Aristotle was asked, "What is the difference between an educated and an uneducated man?" He replied, "The same difference as between being alive and being dead."
–Aristotle

"He not only overflowed with learning, he stood in the slop." –Sydney Smith on Macaulay

"Experience teaches you to recognize a mistake when you've made it again." –Unknown

Keys to Personal Development: Sharing Versus Hoarding

System Manager 1: Hoarding Information

You were the one and only system administrator for two years, but with the growth of the company two more administrators have been hired to work in different divisions.

In the past, information about the system was all in your head and now management is clamoring to have all the information on paper for all to access and use.

You are reluctant to let go of the information, but time passes and the requests for documentation continue, so finally you put the bare minimum on paper. "If they want to know more," you say to yourself, "let them come to a professional to get it."

When the boss comes into one of your meetings with a request for a report on the sharing of system resources you volunteer to write it because you know everything about all the systems and want to be the one to disperse it to the boss, forgetting that you don't really have time to write the report.

The Need For Personal Development

One of the engineers comes to you and mentions that she wants to rework some shell scripts that will save some time for her group.

You strenuously object. You don't want people messing with the system.

"Give me the information," you say, "and I'll do it."

"What do these people think," you say to yourself. "That they can do systems stuff themselves?"

Your boss asks a question at a meeting about porting applications and although one of the other system administrators is in a better position to know the answer, you interrupt and fudge the answer until you can go look it up in the manual. Then you go back and present your boss with the answer.

Administration has been asking you to keep track of the hours you spend in each division. You begin logging the hours in your project software.Other projects distract anyone from checking on your time tracking, and although you continue to track your time, you never pass the information on to administration, figuring you can use it later if you need to make a point in a budget meeting.

System Manager 2: Sharing Information

"You need me to document how the system is laid out and who's on each server? Sure, I'll do that right away."

"Great," you think, "Now I won't have to be called every time something goes wrong, and maybe I can think seriously about taking some time off."

It has always worried you that everything was in your head, but now that there are people to pass the information on to, the company will be a position to make transitions more easily and others can back you up better.

At a meeting with all the staff managers your boss asks you why one of the users crashes her program whenever she uses a particular alias.

"I don't know," you say. "I didn't know she was having trouble. I'll look in to it later today and get back to you."

It may be a problem that you can add to your on-line system for commonly asked questions and problems.

The Primary Goal of Self-Development is Sharing What You Know

What's the difference between Manager 1 and Manager 2?

- Manager 1 holds all cards close to the vest. Manager 2 considers solutions as gifts.

- Manager 1 can't admit he/she doesn't know. Manager 2 assumes he/she doesn't know.

- Manager 1 hates meetings where his/her knowledge might be challenged. Manager 2 considers every new question a challenge.

- Manager 1 is a collector of information. Manager 2 is a disseminator.

Personal development revolves very much around the self. And yet the true test of your development is how your development helps others.

There is a fine line between meditative self-development and proselytizing. Yet for those with confidence in themselves, security in their position, and self-motivation, the fine line is a wide swathe of learning and sharing.

Faced with learning something new, Manager 1 is burdened. Challenged with learning something new, Manager 2 is motivated to master and share.

Facing personal development with an eye toward mastering and sharing opens the door to self-esteem, independence, and advancement.

Getting a Grip on Personal Development

What's important in personal development? Are there tools for developing the self? You bet. There is a whole body of literature on this subject. Here are a few of the pointers that have worked for me:

- The sooner you learn to say I don't know, the sooner you begin to know.

- If you find yourself resisting a body of knowledge, let down your defenses and let the answer find you.

- To reach a career goal you have to build a foundation of knowledge and have the motivation to move forward.

The Need For Personal Development

- If you see your fellow workers as knowledge building blocks and not stepping stones, they will always be there to support you.

- Find a balance between self-sufficiency and time invested to learn things yourself. If you can find expertise elsewhere in less time than you can develop it—hire it.

Summary

☐ Keep a wish list of things you want to master. Make a real effort to master one list item a week.

☐ Practice promoting yourself by sharing knowledge. Test your mastery by how well you can explain something new to another.

☐ Learn to ask questions. The answer is usually in the question.

☐ Listen 60% of the time and talk/act 40% of the time.

☐ Learn to teach without pushing. Avoid condescension at all costs. Develop yourself by developing others. Give others the tools to develop the answer instead of shoving the answer down someone's throat.

The Need For Personal Development

Chapter 7

Technical Mastery Is A Myth

"We do not know one millionth of one percent about anything." –Thomas Alva Edison

"I find that a great part of the information I have was acquired by looking up something and finding something else on the way." –Franklin P. Adams

Chasing the Ultimate System

It seemed like the right thing to do at the time. Your company overhauled its computing system and decided to install a UNIX and PC network. One of your primary responsibilities when they first hired you was to research the options and make a recommendation.

That is exactly what you did. You read the journals, listened to the sales pitches, considered expansion pos-

sibilities, and got estimates. Based on that information you recommended one of the best-known networks as your first choice.

Management agreed with you. Then it became your job to oversee installation and configuration of the network.

You were not prepared for the resistance you met within the company. Most people didn't like the change. They complained about how slow everything ran. What was the point of buying a network if it slowed you down?

Pretty soon everybody in the company was an expert telling you how to do your job. Of course it did not help that 6 months after you bought your network, the vendor came out with a whole new, less costly line of software designed to run on standard PCs instead of proprietary hardware.

Then other vendors came out with perfectly good networking products at a much lower cost. Before long everyone was asking why you did it this way when another way would have been so obviously better. All you could do was wring your hands in despair.

Now you are stuck with a dinosaur the company is still paying off, and everybody blames you!

You Can Never Master It All

The moral to this story is that no matter how well you research a technical solution or how well informed your decisions are, you can still be burned by events beyond your control. In addition, when you work in any high tech industry you always run the risk of being out of date on key technology.

If you do your homework you can minimize the potential of something like this happening. However, you need to recognize one important fact:

- You will never master the technology upon which your system is based.

The simple reason for this is that technology is constantly changing. Mastering it would mean knowing everything about a product before the product developer does.

Making the Best Decision Possible

So, how do you avoid a pitfall like this?

You may not be able to master all the technology or predict the future, but you can learn enough to make informed decisions. More importantly, you can develop a conviction about how the technology applies to your own company's situation.

Another asset in making system management decisions is your own personal experience. In any computer trade journal you are bound to see stories about new technology that, on the face of it, make your systems obsolete. However, experience shows that much of this leading edge technology never catches hold.

The Importance of Defending Your Decisions

In the fast moving computer market there are no absolutely right answers. The best you can do is the best you can do, and you must be prepared to defend that position as technology evolves around you.

In the end, technical mastery is really applying your practical experience with the technology and your knowledge about what's coming to replace it. Technical conviction is applying this mastery to your situation... and defending that decision.

Summary

☐ Keep abreast of technology through the use of self-education, seminars, and publications.

☐ Justify attending user conferences for self-education to higher management. Point out the need to stay current with technology.

☐ Recognize that you'll never understand it all.

☐ When you make a decision about a purchase, don't second guess your decision when newer technology overtakes it. Stand by your convictions.

Chapter 8

Leadership: The Ultimate Act of Independence

"The task of a leader is to get his people from where they are to where they have not been."
–Henry Kissinger

"One hundred thousand lemmings can't be wrong." –Graffito

Taking the Lead

The sales and engineering departments are arguing again. It's the same old competition for necessary resources.

"We have to get this quarterly sales report out today because it has to be ready for the shareholders' meeting. How could you do a kill -9 on my app?"

"And we have to finish the Etheridge project today because tomorrow they start fining us $10,000 a day for every day it's late."

"You guys are nothing without the sales force. No sales, no cash," says the sales guy.

"You guys have nothing to sell without engineering. When are you going to learn that you serve a support function to us?"

"Let's call the boss to set the priority."

It's the same old argument, heated up a bit because of the deadlines.

This really isn't your problem but you wonder if instead of setting one task over the other, you couldn't reallocate resources so that both jobs can meet their deadlines.

You step into the conference room where all the yelling was supposed to be contained.

You say, "What if we reroute the sales server to another network and set the report to print on the high-speed printer in accounting. They are gone for a seminar today. That way you can still get the Etheridge project outputting and run the backup you need later this evening."

Leadership: The Ultimate Act of Independence

"Can you do that fast enough so we can get the report out today?"

"Sure," you say. "This way everybody gets their job done."

"Great. And, really, we only need another hour and a half on the printer in accounting."

"Well, OK. It's a deal."

Managing and Leading

What did the system manager accomplish here? The manager brought solutions to the table and shared them freely, found the good side of a bad situation, recognized and praised. The manager communicated, delegated and educated others about each other's role. This manager led as well as managed.

Who has not wondered how they can be responsible for corporate success? "I'm just one of many," you might think. "Even if I am emerging as an effective manager, can I really make that much of a difference?"

One of the keys is to channel your personal development in a way that sustains and strengthens you. Your company depends on your sustenance just as you depend on your company's success.

Empowering the Lemmings

Your mission as an emerging effective manager is to use your individual strengths to empower yourself and those around you. Collectively you do more than impact the organization. You are the organization.

You must take your growing personal awareness, self-motivation, and comfort with technical mastery and put it to work. As soon as you do, you will see that your expertise and contribution is primarily a catalyst to others.

Making the Jump from "Me" to "Us"

How do you make the jump from "Me" to "Us"? The first step is to recognize the leadership capacity in you.

From your first days in nursery school you've known that it is easier to follow than to lead. Yet everyone has the capacity for leadership. You need to unearth that ability and lead.

"But I'm not a leader," you might say. Have you taken the time to lead yourself to a discovery of personal motivation? Have you worked on your personal development and come to understand your level of technical mastery? If you have—you have lead yourself. That is the first step to leading others.

Summary

☐ Effective leadership is transforming your self-mastery into a catalyst for others.

☐ Leadership is based on a position of strength but not dominance.

☐ Delegating work means delegating responsibility.

☐ Mistakes are natural—recognizing that you are in an indefensible position is hard. Admitting you need help is really tough. Asking others for

One Minute SunSoft Solaris Manager

help is nearly impossible. Getting others to help you when you genuinely ask is easy.

☐ Leadership is letting others make mistakes but not catastrophes.

☐ Whether you are assigned responsibility or you accept it naturally, you need the authority to carry out your responsibility. Try earning it first. Demand it if you must.

☐ Listening is the key tool to leading: listening to yourself and others.

☐ Leadership is sharing and helping. You can't stand by and let others do the wrong thing.

☐ Let others know you are a player; by helping others they will come to value your opinions.

Section 3

Developing The Team

The final step in becoming an effective manager is passing on your knowledge and expertise to others in a way that strengthens the whole organization. We call this stage of interdependent success the "Us" phase. Here you are passing beyond being self-sustaining to being able to sustain others. You control communication, recognition, education, and delegation to, in and through the team to contribute to the corporate mission.

The goal of this section is to move from being one who effectively sustains oneself to one who can pass on these essentials to others. We stress delegation and communication as tools in getting others to work toward corporate success, being an effective team player, putting all these techniques together and finally working toward a corporate mission.

Chapter 9

Helping Others Manage For Your, Their, And Corporate Success

"The boss drives his men; the leader coaches them. The boss depends upon authority; the leader on good will. The boss inspires fear; the leader inspires enthusiasm. The boss says 'I'; the leader 'we.' The boss fixes the blame for the breakdown; the leader fixes the breakdown. The boss says 'go'; the leader says 'let's go!'"–H. Gordon Selfridge

Making Individual Work into Team Work

The project kickoff meeting for the new multimillion dollar government contract is about to begin.

Before you step into the conference room, one of the engineers pulls you aside.

One Minute SunSoft Solaris Manager

"There's a potential problem here," she says. "The specs on this project are unlike anything we've done before. In the past there's been some reluctance to recustomize our environment internally for an outside client."

"O.K.," you say, "Let's bring this up in the meeting and see what solutions we can come up with."

"I don't know," she says. "It may really be opening a can of worms. Maybe we should wait."

The meeting begins. Tasks are broken down and assigned and the milestones are given dates.

Several technical issues are raised and resolved. The chief engineer starts to bring the meeting to a close.

"There's one more thing," you say, catching a worried glance from the engineer who stopped you outside the meeting. "What about the differences in environments between what we use and the government standard. Any ideas about how we can customize without too much effort?"

"We can't, that's how. We aren't set up to change code for every project. We don't have the time or the staff."

"This is our biggest contract; it's time to change in order to stay in the market."

You ask,"How many extra hours would it take to make the changes and wouldn't changing help in bidding for future contracts?"

Several people begin talking at once. You call a halt.

"Let's work out a schedule for getting it done between now and the time this project comes in. Can we get one member from each of your groups to work on this?" you ask.

Slowly, resistance begins to fade and a few people make other suggestions for speeding up the process. The team is working together again and as usual coming up with good ideas.

As the meeting is ending the engineer calls you to the side.

"I'm glad we brought up this problem now. It's going to make a big difference in how smoothly this project runs," she says.

"Yes," you say, "Thanks for raising the issue. It was a good idea to get it solved early."

Stepping into the Management Role

This story illustrates the first step in asserting yourself as a manager in a work group. You must take the risk and the responsibility of stepping forward and laying out what you know in a way that contributes to the goals of the work group.

Effective managers do more than just voice their informed opinions. Managers lead others in a way that cultivates their independence and allows them to fulfill their capabilities.

Enlighten through Delegation

Delegation is more than just a way for you to take control of your time. It serves the work group by distributing tasks to those most able to accomplish them.

Delegation also builds and develops the capabilities, independence and knowledge base of the people around you. This strengthens the team and makes it more productive.

The Art of Letting Loose

The most difficult aspect of management for most burgeoning managers is delegating authority and responsibility as well as tasks. Managers do not like to give up control.

Yet the most effective managers do. They delegate responsibility and authority while keeping themselves available to resolve problems and monitor progress.

Measuring Progress—Staying on Track

You can only give up hands-on control if you have confidence that the tasks you delegate and the direction you give will produce the necessary results. There are several ways to ensure this will happen. Consider these points:

- People take responsibility if you make it clear the responsibility is theirs and if they feel they own a piece of the work.

- You can get people invested in their responsibilities if you work with them to establish their goals.

- Work with people to develop tools that measure progress toward goals, such as deadlines and milestones. The significant contribution of the manager in this process is securing a consensus on these points.

- Establish a reporting system that allows you to monitor progress and be alert to problems others may not foresee.

Summary

☐ You can only become truly independent when you can direct your knowledge, experience and goals through others.

☐ You become successful as a manager when you can give others the tools and guidance they need to manage themselves.

☐ Save yourself from a total "crash and burn" by delegating and managing successfully. You cannot do it all yourself.

☐ You know you are doing it right when everyone in the work group is working together productively and effectively while they achieve personal satisfaction.

Chapter 10

Being An Effective Team Player

"Working with people is difficult, but not impossible." –Peter Drucker

"Never mistake motion for action." –Ernest Hemingway

"A committee is a cul-de-sac down which ideas are lured and then quietly strangled." –Sir Barnnet Cocks

Working With People, Not Against Them

A meeting has been called to assess the status of a project that has missed several milestones. The managers of all the related departments are there.

"How can we get this project back on track?" the chief engineer asks.

"Well if we hadn't lost the central server for so long, we wouldn't have missed the first milestone," says one engineer.

"And if the software architecture was supported on all the machines from the start, we wouldn't be this late."

"And if Joe hadn't quit last month...."

"But the system is up and running now," you say, " my assistant worked out the software problem three weeks ago and sent E-mail around that the problem was fixed, and Joe's replacement starts next week, so let's focus on meeting the next milestone."

The meeting gets back on track, with several suggestions for dividing up the remaining work.

As the meeting is drawing to a close you say,"Does anyone else have other obstacles to getting this job done that we should hear about now? Also, how about if we circulate the project update report to all managers involved from now on?"

Manager as Team Player

What exactly is the manager's role as a team player? It can vary. You may be asked to build a team and then direct its efforts toward a goal, or you may be invited to join an existing team.

No matter how you are involved with the team, one of your essential functions as a team player is a facilitator of communications. An effective team communicator first and foremost listens to the dialog within the work group.

If you are a team leader as well as a participant, your primary role is seeing that the right team members are talking to and hearing each other. Through effective communications, the team taps into the supply of knowledge and resources it possess.

Gathering Resources

Team building is a process of gathering and coordinating resources. Consider these fundamental aspects of building a team:

- To build a team, you must know the ultimate mission of the team.

- Identify resources necessary for accomplishing the mission.

- Line up these resources. Often you cannot have everything you need. Part of the team builder's role is figuring out how to get by with what you have.

- Bring the resources together. The team works to establish its goals and how it will accomplish them.

- If you are a team leader as well as the team builder, your role shifts. You are no longer a manipulator of the resources you have gathered. Instead you promote team work by facilitating communications, listening to the needs of team members and monitoring team progress.

Letting Go

As we mentioned earlier, one of the most difficult tasks for managers is giving up direct control. The effective manager delegates the establishment of

Being An Effective Team Player

goals, solutions and plans to team members. Managers then become team players by contributing their knowledge and experience toward the team's goals and mission.

Tools for Teams

Whether you are a manager leading a team or a manager participating in a team effort, one of your greatest contributions to the team is group communications.

Teams rely on communications to build a consensus, agree on goals, share information, coordinate efforts and stay informed. There are many channels for effective team communications, and they should all be used. They include:

E-mail

- Telephones
- Calendars
- Memos
- Meetings

One Minute SunSoft Solaris Manager

REALITY CHECK: Tremendous amounts of valuable time are routinely frittered away in meetings. Strive for one minute meetings. Set time limits. Keep communications concise and to the point.

Summary

☐ A team's success is due in large part by everyone having a unique role and everyone deferring to each other's expertise.

☐ An effective manager promotes communications within the team and promotes mutual education between team members.

☐ Good communication within the work group is essential for building a consensus around team goals and working out an implementation plan.

☐ Rather than dictating positions, a team leader's major contribution to the team effort is keeping team members focused on goals and drawing the team efforts toward closure.

☐ Never forget, information is a corporate resource that must be made available to everyone.

Chapter 11

Implementing It All

"Leadership is action, not position."–Donald H. McGannon

The Enlightened Manager: A Day in the Life...

8 AM. You sit down at your nearly clean desk and look over the printout of your day's schedule from your scheduling software. This is how it looks:

- 8:30 – Return phone calls to suppliers
- 9:15 – Re-route all lost E-mail
- 9:30 – Meeting on the latest security breach
- 9:50 – Talk to assistant about configuring new machines
- 10:00 – Complete report on additional hardware requirements

One Minute SunSoft Solaris Manager

- 10:45 – Review report and respond to E-mail
- 11:00 – Conference call with system managers at remote sites
- 11:30 – Finish morning schedule
- 12:00 – Lunch with new employee
- 1:00 – Check with assistant on machine configurations; resolve problems
- 1:20 – Order more cable, terminators and anything else you need
- 1:30 – Return phone calls
- 2:00 – Check with accounting that server problems are fixed
- 2:45 – Interview two job applicants
- 3:30 – Review presentation for 4:30 meeting
- 4:30 – Corporate management meeting
- 4:50 – Set up tomorrow's work schedule and return phone calls
- 5:00 – Start Monday backup

Implementing It All

It's a full schedule, but you're on top of it. The first thing you do is check E-mail. There are the usual news items and questions, which you answer as soon as you read them.

You make your phone calls, playing phone tag with two of the suppliers, and head off to the meeting on security. The meeting goes well; all of your suggestions have been considered and several of them have been implemented.

You head directly to the project meeting with the engineers. You help them with a few minor programming problems and the project rolls on.

Your assistant has been working on configuring the new machines, and you stop to check with her that all is going according to the master plan you two worked out ahead of time.

On the way back to your office to complete your report on additional hardware, you are stopped by Jerry in administration.

"I need to get some files transferred to a tape ," he says, "but my tape drive is broken. Can you help? It has to go out by 4:00."

"Sure," you say, "I'll come over about 11:30 and download your files to the tape drive in accounting."

Back in your office you get right to work on the report (after returning the urgent call from your boss, who isn't in). You finish and review the report in time to send some E-mail before placing the conference call to the managers of the remote sites.

When you get off the phone there's another urgent message to call your boss. You call but he's on another line. You leave him an E-mail message and head off to help Jerry transfer his files.

On your way back from helping Jerry you look into your boss' office. He's out to lunch. You check your E-mail and head off to lunch with a new coworker who you want to get to know better.

You check in with your assistant who has run up against a problem with the database conversion. You put your heads together and decide to swap out a few machines with a different department to solve the problem.

You check in with engineering to make sure they aren't getting anymore system errors and then lock yourself into your office to work on a program to run a new document manager.

It's coming along nicely when the first of two job applicants shows up early for the interview. You keep him

Implementing It All

waiting while you finish up the line you're on. The interview goes well and while you are waiting for the other candidate, who is late, you call a couple of references for the first candidate. The second interview comes and goes.

While you are reviewing the presentation for the management meeting at 4:30, you boss sticks his head in the door.

"Good job on the Davo project," he says. "I know you put in a lot of overtime helping to keep that project on schedule."

"My pleasure," you say.

In the management meeting your report is well received and stimulates a productive discussion on resources.

You get back to your desk with just enough time to prepare your schedule for tomorrow and start the backup tape.

At 5:15 you are out the door and on your way to pick up the kids at daycare.

Summary

☐ The need for job security is universal. Knowing this frees you of nurturing your insecurities.

☐ Recognition for a job well done is something we all crave. Make sure to let those around you know you appreciate the occasional pat on the back.

☐ Recognize the need for you to control you own time. If you don't, someone else will.

☐ Job satisfaction is an important aspect of being an effective manager.

☐ Identify what motivates you in a particular task and use it to your advantage.

☐ You are a conduit of information. To be an effective manager you must share your knowledge.

☐ Technology is always on the move. You must continually stay abreast of it. Be prepared to

Implementing It All

defend any hardware or software acquisition with conviction.

☐ Effective leadership is transforming your self-mastery into a catalyst for others.

☐ You can only become truly independent when you can direct knowledge, experience and goals through others.

☐ One of the manager's essential functions as a team player is to facilitate communications.

Chapter 12

Contributing to Corporate Goals and Success

"Do whatever comes your way to do as well as you can. Think as little as possible about yourself and as much as possible about other people and about things that are interesting. Put a good deal of thought into the happiness that you are able to give." –Eleanor Roosevelt

"...the mere resolve not to be useless, and the honest desire to help other people, will, in the quickest and delicatest ways, improve yourself." –John Ruskin

Expanding Your Contribution to the Organization

You've gotten a reputation for being a useful member of the team. A couple of other companies have called recently, asking if you would like to join them. You are grateful for the interest, but you'd like to stay where you are and learn to do better at the new job you've got.

More than the offers from other companies, you are really pleased that your own company has recognized your talents and efforts as well. You have been given a raise and promoted to run all the system departments.

The upper management meetings you have begun to attend have given you a whole new perspective on the overall direction of the company. Now you understand how the recent cutbacks are an effort to regroup for some major contracts coming in. The reasons for the priorities of certain projects are becoming clearer too.

You have a deeper understanding of how the system departments can contribute to the success of the company and a clearer idea of how you can contribute to the performance of your department.

You are beginning to contribute to these upper management meetings with suggestions and questions that will

Contributing to Corporate Goals and Success

ultimately affect how the rest of management sees your department and the allocation of resources.

You have gotten good feedback from the other members of upper management and have passed that on to your staff.

Within your departments you have some new ideas for greater efficiency and the staff to implement them.

You are energized and know how you can work toward increasing the profitability of the company.

More than ever before you feel your worth to the company and know how you can make decisions that will benefit the company. Now the day-to-day problem-solving is connected to the big picture. All is right with the world and your place in it.

Separating Task from Mission

Your ultimate goal as a manager is to contribute to corporate success. To do that you must understand the corporate mission and how you contribute to achieving it.

Understanding the corporate mission enables you to distinguish task from mission. Tasks accomplish the mission. Therefore, tasks should be driven by the mission. This saves you from being driven and consumed by tasks. As you work through your daily barrage of tasks, remember:

- Never loose sight of the mission.

Contributing to the Corporate Mission

The corporate mission is both a guide to you as a manager and the living heart of your enterprise.

As an established, effective, self-confident manager, you can and should contribute to your ever-evolving corporate mission. You possess unique knowledge and expertise that are of great value to the corporate enterprise.

How can you help shape the corporate mission? Through communication and effective action. Engaging in dialog about the corporate mission and working out your own positive contribution to it shapes it dynamically.

Summary

☐ Separate mission from tasks; tasks accomplish the mission.

☐ Understand how your work contributes to the mission.

☐ Get involved in shaping the mission; grow with the mission.

☐ Consider this closing thought:

"Live for another if you wish to live for yourself." –Seneca

One Minute SunSoft Solaris Manager

More OnWord Press Titles

MicroStation Books

INSIDE MicroStation
Book $29.95 Optional Disk $14.95

INSIDE MicroStation Companion Workbook
Book $34.95 Includes Disk/Redline Drawings/Projects

INSIDE MicroStation Companion Workbook Instructor's Guide
Book $9.95 Includes Disk/Redline Drawings/Projects/Lesson Plans

MicroStation Reference Guide
Book $18.95 Optional Disk $14.95

The MicroStation Productivity Book
Book $39.95 Optional Disk $49.95

MicroStation Bible
Book $49.95 Optional Disk $49.95

Programming With MDL
Book $49.95 Optional Disk $49.95

Programming With User Commands
Book $65.00 Optional Disk $40.00

101 MDL Commands
Book $49.95 Optional Executable Disk $101.00 Optional Source Disks (6) $259.95

101 User Commands
Book $49.95 Optional Disk $101.00

Bill Steinbock's Pocket MDL Programmers Guide
Book $24.95

MicroStation for AutoCAD Users
Book $29.95 Optional Disk $14.95

MicroStation for AutoCAD Users Tablet Menu
Tablet Menu $99.95

MicroStation 4.X Delta Book
Book $19.95

The MicroStation 3D Book
Book $39.95 Optional Disk $39.95

Managing and Networking MicroStation
Book $29.95 Optional Disk $29.95

The MicroStation Database Book
Book $29.95 Optional Disk $29.95

The MicroStation Rendering Book
Book $34.95 Includes Disk

INSIDE I/RAS B
Book $24.95 Includes Disk

The CLIX Workstation User's Guide
Book $34.95

SunSoft Solaris Series

The SunSoft Solaris 2.* User's Guide
Book $29.95

SunSoft Solaris 2.* For Managers and Administrators
Book $34.95 Optional Disk $29.95

The SunSoft Solaris 2.* Quick Reference
Book $18.95

Five Steps to SunSoft Solaris 2.*
Book $24.95

One Minute SunSoft Solaris Manager
Book $14.95

SunSoft Solaris for Windows Users
Book $24.95

The Hewlett Packard HP-UX Series

The HP-UX User's Guide
Book $29.95

HP-UX For Managers and Administrators
Book $34.95 Optional Disk $29.95

The HP-UX Quick Reference
Book $18.95

Five Steps to HP-UX
Book $24.95

One Minute HP-UX Manager
Book $14.95

HP-UX for Windows Users
Book $24.95

CAD Management

One Minute CAD Manager
Book $14.95

The CAD Rating Guide
Book $49.00

Geographic Information Systems

The GIS Book
Book $29.95

DTP/CAD Clip Art

1001 DTP/CAD Symbols Clip Art Library: Architectural
Book $29.95

MicroStation
DGN Disk $175.00   Book/Disk $195.00

AutoCAD
DWG Disk $175.00   Book/Disk $195.00

CAD/DTP
DXF Disk $195.00   Book/Disk $225.00

IGES Disk $195.00   Book/Disk $225.00

TIF Disk $195.00 Book/Disk $225.00

EPS Disk $195.00 Book/Disk $225.00

HPGL Disk $195.00 Book/Disk $225.00

CD ROM With All Formats
CD $275.00 Book/CD $295.00

Networking/LANtastic

Fantastic LANtastic
Book $29.95 Includes Disk

The LANtastic Quick Reference
Book $14.95

One Minute Network Manager
Book $14.95

OnWord Press Distribution

End User/Corporate

OnWord Press books are available worldwide to end users and corporate accounts from your local bookseller or computer/software dealer or call 1-800-223-6397 or 505/473-5454.

Wholesale

Domestic Education

OnWord Press books are distributed to the US domestic education market by Delmar Publishers. Call 518/464-3569,

Fax 518/464-0301 or write Delmar Publishing Inc. at Two Computer Drive West, Albany, NY 12212.

Domestic Trade

OnWord Press books are distributed to the US domestic trade by Van Nostrand Reinhold. Call 1-800-842-3636, Fax 606/525-7778 or write Van Nostrand Reinhold at 7625 Empire Drive, Florence, KY 41042.

Europe, Middle East, and Africa

OnWord Press books are distributed in Europe, the Middle East, and Africa by International Thomson Publishing. Call 071-497-1422, Fax 071-494-1426 or write International Thomson Publishing at Berkshire House, 168-173 High Holborn, London WC1V 7AA, United Kingdom.

Asia, Pacific, Hawaii, Puerto Rico, and South America

OnWord Press books are distributed in Asia, the Pacific, Puerto Rico, and South America by Thomson International Publishing. Call 415/598-0784, Fax 415/598-9953 or write Thomson International Publishing at 10 Davis Drive, Belmont, CA 94002.

OnWord Press, 1580 Center Drive, Santa Fe, NM 87505 USA